TOP TIPS:
DISCOVERING THE BIBLE
WITH CHILDREN

Terry Clutterham and John Stephenson

Copyright © Scripture Union 2009
First published 2009
ISBN 978 184427 335 5

Scripture Union England and Wales
207-209 Queensway, Bletchley, Milton
Keynes, MK2 2EB, England
Email: info@scriptureunion.org.uk
Website: www.scriptureunion.org.uk

Scripture Union Australia
Locked Bag 2, Central Coast Business
Centre, NSW 2252
Website: www.scriptureunion.org.au

Scripture Union USA
PO Box 987, Valley Forge, PA 19482
Website: www.scriptureunion.org

The right of Terry Clutterham and
John Stephenson to be identified as
authors of this work has been
asserted by them in accordance with
the Copyright, Designs and Patents
Act 1988.

British Library Cataloguing-in-
Publication Data: a catalogue record
of this book is available from the
British Library.

Printed and bound in Singapore by
Tien Wah Press Ltd.

Logo, cover design, internal design:
www.splash-design.co.uk

Internal illustrations: Colin Smithson

Typesetting: Richard Jefferson, Author
and Publisher Services

Advisers: John Grayston, Alison Hendy,
John Marshall

🐌 Scripture Union is an
international Christian charity working
with churches in more than 130
countries, providing resources to bring
the good news about Jesus Christ to
children, young people and families
and to encourage them to develop
spiritually through the Bible and
prayer.

As well as our network of volunteers,
staff and associates who run holidays,
church-based events and school
Christian groups, we produce a wide
range of publications and support
those who use our resources through
training programmes.

CONTENTS

INTRODUCTION

Just think. The almighty God, the awe-inspiring Creator of everything and everyone, who is above and beyond all time, space and place, wants to speak with Abigail, Chung, Farrah and Andreas, the children in your care. He has some very important news to tell them. He longs for them to know him. He wants to let them in on all his plans, and to draw them into his work of bringing people back to himself. 'God himself revealed his mysterious plan to me' (Ephesians 3:3 NLT).

Christian educator, Lawrence Richards, calls the Bible, 'God's invitation to us to experience reality'. The children in the Narnia stories venture through the wardrobe and find themselves in a world that's far more 'real' than this one. Your children can discover through the Bible that there is something far more 'real', more important and more lasting than PlayStations, the Simpsons and MSN – it's the reality of God at work, often in strange, secret and very profound ways. When children gain confidence with the Bible, this wonderful world will open up to them, and they will catch their breath in wonder.

Discovering the Bible with children is not just about enjoying the great stories together, as important as that is – it's about encouraging children to say, 'Yes' to God with their whole lives. Easy to say, not so easy to do. The Bible and children seem not to be made for each other. How will they ever get into such a big and difficult book? *Top Tips on Discovering the Bible with children* is here to help!

Our own enthusiasm for the Bible and for the difference it makes to us will be infectious! That's why we start with what the Bible says about itself. Don't skip this part! Then we'll focus on some useful guidelines for discovering the Bible with children, before getting down to some practical ideas that we can use, adapt and develop to suit the children we know. We hope that this book will help all children's workers stay true to the Bible and true to the children themselves in our expectations and hopes for them.

PART ONE – CLUES FROM THE BIBLE

Not surprisingly, the clues about how to discover the Bible with children are best found within the Bible itself.

The Bible comes from God

'All Scripture is God-breathed…' (2 Timothy 3:16). God inspired (breathed into) the people who wrote it. He gave them the Holy Spirit (breath). What was in God's mind – the thoughts, plans, truths, warnings and promises – got into them. They then said it in their own way. What they wrote came from God.

> **Think about…**
> Find 2 Timothy 3:15–17 and make two lists:
> What these verses tell me about the Bible.
> What the Bible is for.
> How might each of these observations affect the way I handle the Bible with children, or the way they handle it for themselves?

No one comes face to face with God and stays the same. As we explore the Bible with children, we can all expect to hear from God himself through it and therefore to be changed. Never open the Bible with children if you want a nice, quiet, predictable time. Exploring the Bible is a spiritual activity with life-changing, possibly world-changing consequences!

The Bible is an extraordinary book

It's not one book, but 66. Look at the contents page of your own Bible. There are two Testaments, 'Old' and 'New' – 39 books in the Old Testament, 27 in the New. 40 or more different writers wrote the 1189 chapters of the Bible, except they didn't originally write the books with chapter breaks – those came much later!

Most of the Old Testament was written in Hebrew (the ancient language of the people of Israel). A few parts were in Aramaic which was the 'international', conversation language of the Middle East, dating from Old Testament times, and later becoming the language Jesus spoke. Greek was the main language used for the New Testament. 'Testament' means 'covenant' or 'agreement' between God and people – the old covenant was based on the laws God gave his people, the Jews, and the new, on having faith in Jesus.

The Bible is the true story of God saving his people through Jesus

Amazingly, with so many writers and covering around 2,100 years of the history of the Middle East, the Bible makes up one big, true story. God created people to belong to him, but right at the start, in the Garden of Eden, they thought they knew better than him and rejected him. The rest of the Bible is about how God made a people of his own, the Jewish nation, and then sent Jesus to die so that everyone – not only Jews but also the rest of the world – can belong to him. At the end of everything, in heaven, 'They will be his people, and God himself will be with them and be their God' (Revelation 21:3).

The Bible has many different types of writing in it

God has chosen to reveal his big plan through many different kinds of writing – stories and histories, law, words of wisdom, poetry, song, prophecy, Gospel episodes, letters or epistles, and visionary writings. In these different ways, the Bible is rich and colourful, moving and shocking, enthralling and hard-hitting, easy and difficult. Children need to read all these styles of writing in slightly different ways, to understand them properly.

When we say, 'The Bible is true,' what do we mean? From the historical writings in the Bible, 'it's true' will mean the events actually took place; in poetry, the phrases, verses and images help us grasp and respond to the truth about God; in epistles, we find true teaching about God and about the way he wants his people to live. The Bible certainly is true, but in many different ways.

> **In reality...**
> 'God has feathers!' Christina chirped up. When asked how she knew this, she said, 'Psalm 36:7 says, "People take refuge in the shadow of your wings." If God has wings, he must have feathers!' There followed an intriguing discussion about the nature of poetry and how not all the words in the Bible can be taken at face value...

The Bible helps faith in God to grow

The apostle Paul wrote, 'All Scripture … is useful for teaching, rebuking, correcting and training in righteousness, so that all God's people may be thoroughly equipped for every good work' (2 Timothy 3:16,17). Thomas Groome wrote, 'All people have faith in different ways.' (*Christian Religious Education: Sharing Our Story and Vision*, San Francisco: Harper and Row, 1980). But what does that mean?

There's believing faith (for instance, 'I believe there's a heaven'). This grows by discovering more from the Bible about how God says things are ('teaching') and how he doesn't want them to be ('rebuking').

There's trusting faith (for instance, 'I trust the Lord Jesus with my whole life'). This grows when we become God's people ('salvation through faith in Christ Jesus' (2 Timothy 3:15)) and discover in the Bible more and more reasons to love and trust him.

There's doing faith (for instance, 'I'm going to step out in faith, and forgive and make friends with her'). This grows by seeing how God wants things to be in our life ('correcting and training in righteousness').

There's our will, our determination to go God's way (for instance, 'I always want to be and do what God wants'). This grows by seeing all that God has done, is doing and all the Bible tells us he will do, and by wanting to play a part in it ('equipped for every good work').

Another way of describing these aspects of faith is 'head, hearts and hands faith'. As children discover the Bible, God nurtures all-round, multifaceted faith. We'll discover more of this on page 20. 'Dear brothers and sisters, we can't help but thank God for you, because your faith is flourishing and your love for one another is growing' (2 Thessalonians 1:3, NLT).

PART TWO – BASIC GUIDELINES

2

About us

We are role models

Research tells us that the top reason why people (including children) start reading the Bible is that someone else raves about it. Their enthusiasm and authentic experience are catching.

In reality...

Percy ran a weekly boys' Bible club for me and three others. Percy seemed about 300 years old, but he can't have been! He gave me my love for the Bible. Week by week, we sat around the old kitchen table while he talked us through the events and teachings of the Bible, keeping us busy looking up verses and simply telling us stories of what these truths meant in his own life. He loved his dog-eared Bible with its spidery biro handwriting all over it and creased, torn pages – evidence enough that here was a book he adored, about a God who was as real as could be. I was hooked.

We are learners

We never stop learning from the Bible, because God never stops wanting to speak. Along with the children we care for, we too will continue to be surprised with something new from the Bible.

Think about…

To be equipped as role model, learner and clarifier, explore the Bible every day for yourself. Go to www.wordlive.org for a flexible, multi-media approach to the Bible that lets you choose how, where and when you read it. See page 32 for details.

We are clarifiers

Inevitably children will ask us hard questions about the Bible. We need to make things clear for them. We have three choices – either we honestly say, 'I don't know but I'll find out for you', or we don't know but, with the children, we both agree to find out and compare answers (which affirm their insights) or we do know and we tell them. If we only do the first, we send out the message that the book we claim to want children to read is completely unknown to us, or is tough to understand.

About children

We can let them be themselves

God can speak to children too! We can invite them to tell us what they see and hear in the Bible. We can encourage them to ask questions, and try to answer their own and others' questions. Of course we can check that their comments line up with what's actually in the Bible. Children will often see the obvious thing we have missed, or the hard thing we hoped they would miss!

We can help them become skilful Bible handlers

Some children struggle with reading, but we want all children to become skilful Bible handlers, listening to and engaging with its message even if they can't or won't read! Handling the Bible involves not only the 'big book' itself, but also the 'big God-thoughts' contained in it (the 'theology'). This *Top Tips* book not only provides ways to simply tell children what is in the Bible, but also activities that will help them discover and experience it for themselves. To find out more, read *Top Tips on Communicating God in non-book ways (SU)*.

In reality…
On a wide-open, grassy area, children and adults together measured out Noah's boat. It might rain. Markers in the ground showed the awesome size of the thing. We sat huddled together like Noah's family in the middle to hear the story from the Bible. Then we discussed, 'What kind of God do we have?' The discussion was inspiring. And it didn't rain!

About the Bible

Anticipation
We can help children discover that this is no ordinary book. This might mean pausing to pray with them before we read it or sharing stories of occasions when God spoke and things changed. However, it's not a magical book, like a Harry Potter book of spells – it's what God says through it and how he changes us by it that counts.

Letting the Bible speak for itself
The Bible comes with the authority of God. It has clarity and power. Sometimes it will speak for itself, so we won't need to teach it. For this to happen, the children need a Bible version they can easily understand. Children should be encouraged to listen carefully. Something visual or

In reality…

The service organiser asked a carpenter in the church to make a rough wooden cross, about the size to hold a person. As the all-age congregation listened to the story of the crucifixion from the Bible, the cross was raised up. Everyone wrote their name on a slip of paper. Then they dropped their name at the foot of the cross. It might mean nothing or everything, as somehow they connected themselves and their life with what took place two thousand years ago – or chose not to.

some non-distracting background music sometimes helps focus attention.

Bible versions

Some Bible versions are more suitable for children than others. For under-5s, it's more appropriate to use an illustrated book that vividly and faithfully retells Bible stories. *The Big Bible Storybook* (SU) is ideal. For older children, the *Contemporary English Version* is clear and simple, and for early secondary years, the *Good News Bible* and *Youth Bible (New Century Version)* help with more abstract concepts.

Hearing, seeing, reading

Should children hear, see, or read the Bible passage for themselves, or a combination of all three? This depends on reading abilities. If reading or even following the words will be a

stumbling block to focusing on what the words are actually saying, it is better to just listen. In fact, for people of any age, listening to the Bible read well can have a tremendous impact.

Remembering
'My eyes stay open through the watches of the night, that I may meditate on your promises' (Psalm 119:148). It is important that children carry on thinking about what they have heard from God. This is Bible meditation. In Latin, the word meditatio means 'a pondering or thinking over, and over and over and over'. A time of Bible discovery should be memorable, so that not only the fun of it stays with the children, but also the very heart of the Bible message. A traditional way of doing this is to encourage children to learn and repeat Bible verses by heart, but there are other ways too, as we'll see on page 23.

One big story
Why is it important for children to discover the big story of salvation that is found in the Bible? Firstly, knowing the big story places Jesus firmly at the centre. He is the most important person, making all the rest happen. Secondly, the big story helps children grasp the meaning of individual stories as they connect them with the big one. Thirdly, for children to know what it involves to be lifelong followers of God, they need to see where they now fit in the big story and where God is heading. See page 19 for what this might mean in practice.

Different kinds of writing
There are many different styles (or genres) of writing in the Bible. Poetry stimulates our imagination and engages our emotions; with narrative (story) we grasp the characters, plot and motivations, the beginning, middle and end; prophecy and song often present us with images; law involves understanding history, and so on. There's no one way to explore the Bible but we need to help children distinguish the different styles of writing, and that can be a challenge!

Different learning styles

Even more variety is introduced when we realise that children have different strengths and preferences in learning. Some prefer tactile (touch) approaches; others auditory (hearing), visual (sight), or kinaesthetic (physical action) ways. In *Frames of Mind* (1983) and *Multiple Intelligences* (1993), Howard Gardner broadens the range of learning styles to music, logic, body (physical activity), people (interacting with others), word, environment, visual and self (reflection). All children are intelligent in one or more of these ways, so all styles are important approaches to the Bible.

Growing faith

It is vital to have plenty of activities to help them grow in their thinking about and believing in God, in loving and trusting him and in living differently in God's way. Variety isn't just making sure they don't get bored but stimulates all aspects of 'head, heart and hands faith'.

PART THREE – PRACTICAL IDEAS

3

Find time for 'Bible chat'

Chat with the children about your own experience with the Bible, and about theirs too. Make it a natural, relaxed part of your relationship with them. The Bible isn't just a book – it's the way for us all to hear God's Word, which is 'alive and active' (Hebrews 4:12). Accept what the children have experienced with the Bible and be non-judgemental about what they haven't. Always be positive, encouraging them to explore the Bible more and more in the future, being ready to hear God's Word.

The kinds of message you'll want to convey in your chat are:
- 'The Bible is from God. It's valuable' – to encourage a positive attitude towards the Bible.
- 'I want to hear from God about God through it' – to give motivation.
- 'The Bible is also about me' – to stimulate their interest.

(In 1999, Mazzoni, Gambrell and Korkeamaki researched ways of encouraging children to start reading. Their report, called *Reading Attitudes and Literacy Skills in Prekindergarten and Kindergarten Children*, published by Springer Netherlands, is available as a download from http://www.springerlink.com/content/c76wm34hpqg479jt/. They discovered that if children have the right attitude, motivation and interest, they'll want to read. The same would be true for older children too, and in relation to the Bible.

Allow children time to respond

Encourage children to respond to a Bible passage in their own way, without rushing to satisfy your own agenda. What is this story/passage all about? Why was it written? How does it fit with the big story (see page 19)? What effect did God want it to have on the people who first heard it? It's important to explore all this with children. They may make other observations that are perfectly in line with what the rest of the Bible says, and which may not be quite the way we would see or say it. Children's contributions help us all to learn. That is why listening skills are so vital in children's work.

So, after children have heard or read the Bible passage, pause with them. Ask the following kinds of questions, not looking for that one right answer:

- What do you think this tells us about God?
- How do you feel after hearing that?
- Why do you think this happened?
- What do you want to say to God now?

Children will make connections between the Bible and life, and they may respond to those connections with awe and wonder, prayer, praise, action, confession or thanksgiving. They may relate the Bible passage to something that's happening in their own lives, or they may just see what God is doing and apply it for everyone. Let the Holy Spirit work.

Use multi-sensory ways to 'read' the Bible

Long before they can read, children can listen to the Bible. The events and teachings of the Bible were passed on by word of mouth long before they were written down. However, it's important for children to grasp that these words come from the Bible book, so make sure they can see your Bible, the source of authority. Looking at

pictures of the Bible events helps to stimulate their imagination. When the children are comfortable with recognising printed words, they can hear it and follow it at the same time. Encourage more confident readers to read it for themselves, either silently, or aloud in pairs or to the group.

Encourage active listening

Before they hear a Bible passage, encourage children to listen actively for certain things. If you have a group of children, divide them into teams. Each team listens out for something different. In the story of David and Goliath (1 Samuel 17) they might listen for: clues about Goliath; clues about David; clues about God. Each team feeds back, so that the whole group gains a fuller understanding.

Provide Bible navigation tools

- Hand out Bibles.
- Introduce the contents page, with all the Bible books and page numbers listed and show them how to find a Bible book in the list.
- Turn to the first page number at the start of a Bible book. You may even have to explain about columns.

- Point out the big numbers on the page – chapters – and the smaller ones – verses.
- Explain how Bible references work, for instance, Deuteronomy 5:1–5, means Deuteronomy chapter five, beginning to read at verse 1 and going through to the end of verse 5.
- Avoid the temptation of making it a race to find the place. Some children will always be left behind and may start to feel bad about the whole Bible experience.

Introduce simple Bible meditation

Use the following simple pattern with children, based on lectio divina (divine/spiritual/holy reading), an ancient devotional method:
- Encourage children to settle down alone, ready to listen to what God might want to say to them.

In reality...
Most of my team members thought I was crazy to try anything reflective with a lively group of ten-year-old boys. They sat around the edge of the room in their own spaces. I challenged them not to giggle or disrupt each other but to focus on the Bible and on God. The first time was a total disaster – they simply couldn't do it. But, the fifth time, judging by their reactions and questions afterwards, I'm sure God spoke to them. The team had a better grasp of the importance of introducing quiet God-ward reflection into the lives of busy children.

- First they read the Bible verses slowly and silently (or hear them) several times, allowing the words to sink in.

- If a particular word or phrase catches their attention, they can stop reading or listening.
- Silently they repeat the phrase a few times.
- Next they tell or ask God about what has come to mind.
- They can say the Lord's Prayer, making sure they can see the words if they don't know them already.
- Then they read the Bible verses again. You may wish to follow this with a Bible chat time, for as long as is appropriate – see page 15. But don't force them to share their reflections.

Set the scene

There are many historical, cultural and geographical references in the Bible that children won't be familiar with, but which are important for them to grasp, such as 'What is a Pharisee?' and 'What kind of river is the Jordan?' Give them as much detailed information as appropriate. Then the Bible is more likely to speak for itself.

For instance, for children to begin to think about the parable of the good Samaritan, they need to know what a 'Samaritan' is. Call him 'the traveller's enemy' and 'the enemy of the listening crowd', or do much more to help them understand the history of the Jewish-Samaritan hatred.

Grasp the big story

It is important for children to grasp the big story. Write each of the following phrases on a separate card:

God creates; sin spoils; people wander; Jesus dies; Jesus lives; Jesus in heaven; Spirit comes; Church grows; us now; Jesus returns.

Distribute the cards for the children to illustrate. Use the cards in order as prompts to teach the big story so that the children can say it by heart. Jumble the cards and invite children to arrange them in the right order. Finally, hide the cards and tell the story together unprompted. Regularly display the cards in your room. Whenever you discover a new part of the Bible with the children, write the Bible story title on a Post-it note, and stick it to the appropriate card.

Think about five stories all running in parallel

These five different layers of story help children, prompted by the Holy Spirit, to make good connections between the Bible and life:
- God's story (the big story of the Bible)
- the Bible story itself (the actual narrative)
- the children's own story (they 'tell' the story of what's happening in their own life, that has any connection with the Bible events)
- our own story (how God has used this part of the Bible to change our lives)
- the story of other Christians (what is going on in our own church or on a national scale, or examples of Christians through history) that relate to these events or to the God-truths behind them.

Think carefully about the questions you ask

The following question suggestions are based on the triple response of head (intellectual), heart (emotional) and hand (active). People of all ages benefit from responding to God in all three ways.

Ask big questions (head faith)
When working with one or more children, challenge their faith with more stretching questions such as:
- From this Bible story, who is God?

- What is God like in these verses?
- What has he done?
- Or what is he doing?
- Or what will he do?
- What does God want and what doesn't he want?
- What will it be like to live with this God?
- What do you want to say to God now?

Such questions can open up children's thinking about God – and encourage awe and wonder – rather than closing it down by simply getting them to give the 'right answers'. Tough questions challenge children to work out their answer to the one question, 'What difference might it make to us?'

Simpler questions such as the following can help build all-round faith:

- Head: From this story, is there something new for us to believe about God? Is there another story in the Bible that helps us understand the same thing about God?
- Heart: How does this story make you feel? Why? Can you see any new reason in this story to love and trust God? Is there something special you want to say to God?
- Hands: From this story, is there something you want to do for God or that God wants you to do?

Children of course ask faith-building questions themselves, questions for clarification, trying to make connections, or simple curiosity!

Encourage frequent encounters (heart faith)

Reading the Bible every day can help children store up evidence and reasons why they can trust God with their whole lives. Children don't have to read the Bible daily out of a sense of fear or duty, but out of a love for it and for God, although they do like routine! Maybe once a day won't be enough!

> **In reality…**
> One group of children got so used to asking big questions about God and life, such as, 'Will there be dogs in heaven?' that their church took their questions seriously and built an adult sermon series around them.

For over-5s, go to your local Christian bookshop or national Scripture Union website to find out which Bible reading guide would best suit your children. The church may need to budget to buy them for the group too. Have a Bible time with your children as a model, until they feel sufficiently confident with it to do it on their own. This is especially important for those who don't come from church families or whose parent(s) are new to the Christian faith. If you have a group, try using 10 or 15 minutes each time you meet for them to get used to doing their individual Bible time, with you being available to help.

Ask questions to take children on a journey (hands faith)

Children themselves are on a faith journey and you are travelling with them. Of course, many Bible stories involve journeys. Help children

'enter into' the story by using a mix of mapping, storytelling, imagining, acting, chatting and other fun activities. For example, discovering the story of one of Paul's journeys (Acts 21:1–16), check out a map of the Mediterranean. Decide which direction in your room will be north, and place name labels on the floor to represent the very rough geographical locations of Cos, Patara, Cyprus, Tyre, Ptolemais, Caesarea and Jerusalem.

As you read out the Bible verses, take a small group of children with you from one place to the next as each town is mentioned, and act out and talk about what happens there. Draw out the learning and the application as you travel, asking relevant questions, such as: 'What does that tell us about God?', 'Have you ever been in a situation like that?', 'What do you think you would want God to do if you …?'

Explore the Five S's

The following activities are based on what is known as the 'Five S's' – non-book ways of helping children learn and remember the Bible. The five ways are: Song; Story; Slogan; Symbol (image); Scheme (action). Visit www.unlockurban.org.uk/about.php for more details.

Psalm painting (Song)

Poetry is a work of art, full of colour, mood, image and movement. Children can respond to poetry using other artistic media, for instance, paint. Read a psalm aloud a few times, and let the children paint what they 'see' in their mind's eye, using colours and texture to suit the mood, patterns to express any repeated words, phrases or concepts, and include any images the psalmist uses. Is it a happy psalm? Is God angry? Overall, does the psalm seem to be about God's love? By all means prompt with questions like these, but let the children paint freely as you read. Give the children the opportunity to show and tell about their painting, but don't pressurise them into it.

God song (Song)

The Bible is God-focused – it tells us who he is, what he is like, and what he wants us to do in response. After discovering part of the Bible with the children, make up a simple song about him. You may like to use the tune of a well-known Christian song or chorus and create a new verse, or simply use a rhythm. For instance, start a clapping accompaniment – one, two, pause; one, two, pause:

> (Two claps as you shout out) God is… (then pause until someone offers a word or two to describe God from the Bible verses).
> God is… (word or phrase).
> God is… (word or phrase).
> (All together after the third line, this time with four slower claps) Thank you, Father God.

Then run it all together as a 'seamless' song. Repeat the pattern until the children run out of words!

Entering in (Story)

Help children to 'enter in' to the Bible story to identify with the characters. They can see 'first-hand' what it is like to live in an environment where God is clearly at work.

When reading or retelling a Bible story, pause occasionally, though not so much that you ruin the flow of the narrative. Choose 'before-', 'during-' and 'after-the-action moments' for your pauses and questions. Here is an example, using the story of Peter and the unproductive fishing trip (John 21):

Peter and his friends went fishing one night. They were out in their boat all night, but they didn't catch any fish. It was getting close to breakfast time. (How do you think Peter and his friends felt about this?)

A man called out from the beach, 'Have you caught any fish yet?' Peter and his friends called back to him, 'No, not yet.' 'Try the other side of the boat and you will find some,' the man called. (What do you think Peter and his friends thought of this man?)

They put out the net on the other side of the boat. They could hardly pull the net in because it was so full. It had 153 fish in it. (How might Peter and his friends have felt now?)

The man was Jesus. Peter and his friends had seen Jesus die, but here he was alive again!

Think about...

'Literary history gave us moral fables. We don't need the Bible to teach children moral lessons. We need the Bible to introduce children to God, God's story, and God's ways' (Ivy Beckwith *Postmodern Children's Ministry: Ministry to Children in the 21st Century*).

Sum-up slogan (Slogan)

Sum up in a shout or slogan the main teaching from a Bible passage. Then encourage the children to learn it, and repeat it often.

For instance, learning from the story of Jesus' death and his words 'It is finished!' can be summed up as follows:

'Jesus took the punishment for sin,

once (action of holding up one finger),

for all (action of pointing round with the same finger to everyone present),

and for all time (action of drawing circles in the air with the same finger).'

Teach it during the story, use it twice more later on in the story, then use it again as a 'response':

'That Jesus died,
once (action),
for all (action),
and for all time (action),
so that we can be your friends, Lord, we thank you.'

Paint or draw 1 (Symbol)

As you read a Bible story two or three times, invite the children to draw or paint what particularly strikes them, with no further prompting. If you  are in a group, look appreciatively at all the paintings or drawings, and check out what has made the biggest impression on the group, according to the number of times it is depicted.

Ask why they chose that particular thing to draw or paint. Was anything in the story overlooked?

Paint or draw 2 (Symbol)

Read the Bible passage twice or three times. Encourage the children to imagine they're there. Allow time for them to draw or paint what they can see happening. Then ask them: 'So what is happening that we can't see?' This last question might help them to look behind the action to what God is doing in it.

> **In reality…**
>
> Often in an all-age learning time, I'll choose three of the five S's (Song, Story, Slogan, Symbol or Scheme) to help everyone explore a Bible passage using the most appropriate approaches for the style of Bible writing. For instance, we learn the main point once visually, once in a story and once with an action. I'm not teaching three different things, but the same thing three times, so that people with different learning preferences can grasp the learning at the heart of the Bible passage.

Serious play (Scheme)

Children learn through play. There's no reason why they have to just sit still and listen while a Bible story is being told. If they 'play' with Bible stories, they can internalise them better and act out their meanings more easily.

For example, take *Godly Play*, devised by Jerome Berryman. It is a popular approach to Bible storytelling. It involves a storyteller and a group exploring a Bible story together in a close community. During a standardised *Godly Play* session, the storyteller prepares the group for a time of reflection in their 'sacred place' and then follows a script to tell the story. He or she tells the story visually, using a variety of objects – artefacts, candles, fabric, wooden figures. This is followed by open questions and discussion, especially using 'I wonder…' type prompts. It is made clear that there are no right answers, but children are encouraged to make connections for themselves with other stories and understandings. Every contribution is accepted.

The children respond to the story in any way they like, using art, making puzzles, silence, further play with the artefacts and writing. Everyone then enjoys food together (a 'feast'). Each child leaves with a personal blessing from the storyteller.

Create Bible memories

Children absorb vivid reminders of their learning in word, image, story, song or fun activity. With these they carry more of God's Word with them as they go. What will prompt them to recall their learning will be:

- a vivid story they heard that fascinated them or maybe connected with their own life story
- a fun activity they did with their friends through which they discovered something new from the Bible
- a repeated phrase that somehow summed up the heart of what they heard from God
- a clear picture in their mind's eye or a small scrap of paper with a doodle folded up in their pocket
- a song that is Bible words, for instance from Scripture Union's *Bitesize Bible Songs* for 5 to 11s.

Think about...

'A memory is what is left when something happens and does not completely unhappen.' (Edward de Bono).

These memories help them chew over the Bible words, hum or say them to themselves on the beach or on the sports field, until God's Word does its work in them, as a flower unfolds its petals (one of the meanings of the Hebrew word for meditation).

Encourage all-age Bible learning

Children and adults help each other to meet with God through the Bible. This is not just true for adults who lead a children's group, but parents and family members too. In all-age services and family events, look for ways to encourage mutual Bible engagement. This may mean showing parents how to read the Bible with their children. It may also mean making available suitable resources.

Look for the opportunities in school

The Bible is not just an important book for Christians. It is foundational for those of other faiths and those with no faith. As such it has influenced our culture to affect education, politics, literature, science, music and more. So studying the Bible

gives insight into the society we live in. There are many opportunities to engage with the world of education – bringing insight and understanding about the influence of the Bible in shaping our world.

Think about...
Explore what you might do in your local school. Look on the back cover to find out about the *Into the Bible* project and the opportunities to use it in schools.

Think about...
'Jesus said, "I praise you, Father, Lord of heaven and earth, because you have hidden these things from the wise and learned, and revealed them to little children. Yes, Father, for this was your good pleasure"' (Matthew 11:25,26).

TEN TOP TIPS

- Before opening a particular part of the Bible with children, let it do its work on you first, so that you have your own story to tell.

- Expect God to speak to children. Listen to what he has to teach you through them.

- Make each time of Bible exploration with a group or with an individual child fun, warm, encouraging and inviting.

- Handle the Bible book as much as you can when you retell Bible stories. Then the children will know that this is where the stories come from and this is the 'book God has given us'.

- As soon as they are able, help children gain the skills to handle the Bible book for themselves.

- In age-appropriate ways, encourage children to connect the individual story from the Bible with the big story of God, Jesus and the salvation of the world.

- Re-introduce quiet, Bible-focused time into children's busy lives.

- Use a combination of song, story, slogan, scheme and symbol, to help Bible memories stick.

- Learn key Bible verses by heart with children, building up to a core of perhaps 30 that the children continue to use regularly.

- Pray earnestly for the children in your care to stay listening to God through the Bible their whole lives long.

RESOURCES

Children and the Bible

Victoria Beech, *Bitesize Bible Songs* (2006) and *Bitesize Bible Songs 2* (2008), Scripture Union – CD and downloads at www.scriptureunion.org.uk

Jerome Berryman, *Teaching Godly Play*, The Sunday Morning Handbook, Abingdon Press, 1995

Terry Clutterham, *The Adventure Begins*, Scripture Union/CPAS, 1996

Rachel Coupe, *The Scripture Union Bible Timeline*, Scripture Union, 2008

Maggie Barfield, *Big Bible Story Timeline*, Scripture Union, 2008

Rosemary Cox, *Using the Bible with Children*, Grove Books Limited, 2000

Robert Willoughby, *Children's Guide to the Bible* (for 8–11s), Scripture Union, 1998

Kathryn Copsey and Jean Elliott, *Top tips on Communicating God in non-book ways*, Scripture Union, 2007

Terence Copley, *The Story of the Book*, Scripture Union, 2005

Children and faith development

Ivy Beckwith, *Postmodern Children's Ministry*, Zondervan, 2004

Cecily Cupit, *Come and Follow Jesus*, Scripture Union Australia, 2006

The Bible in schools

Into the Bible: 101 Routes to Explore (for 8–11s), Scripture Union, 2007

The Barnabas Schools' Bible, BRF, 2007

Learning styles

Howard Gardner, *Frames of Mind: The Theory of Multiple Intelligences*, BasicBooks, 1983 and *Multiple Intelligences: The Theory in Practice*, BasicBooks, 1993

Marlene Lefever, *Learning Styles: Reaching Everyone God Gave You to Teach*, Colorado Springs: Cook, 2002
P Honey and A Mumford, *Manual of Learning Styles*, 1986

Adult Bible reading

www.wordlive.org, by Scripture Union
Other Scripture Union titles to help adults get to grips with the Bible: *Bible Max* (exploring larger chunks of the Bible at a time, keeping a journal); *Daily Bread* (practical biblical living); *Encounter with God* (study approach); *Closer to God* (reflective approach); *Wise Traveller* (spiritual journeying with the Bible).

Retold Bible stories

The Big Bible Storybook (for under 5s), Scripture Union, 2007
Alexander Brown, *The Green Book of Must Know Stories* (for 5–7s), Scripture Union, 2008,
Alexander Brown, *The Red Book of Must Know Stories* (for 5–7s), Scripture Union, 2008
Heather Butler, *The 10 Must Know Stories*, Scripture Union, 2008